Secret Agent Hillary
and the Case of the Missing Hotdog

Written by Beth Schaefer
Illustrated by Hasby Mubarok

Dedicated to my kickass, powerhouse nieces,
Sadie and Madeline

Absurdist Fiction: A genre that focuses on the experiences of characters in situations where they cannot find any inherent purpose in life, most often represented by meaningless actions. Elements include satire, dark humor, incongruity, and controversy regarding the condition of being "nothing."

Books on a Whim
Copyright 2016
Evanston
ISBN: 978-0-578-17052-7
BooksOnAwhim.com

Hillary loved being Senior Sergeant. She loved catching criminals. She loved saving lives. She loved working with Assistant Sergeant Macy.

But she longed to be an investigator. You see, Hillary had more than brawn, she had brains.

One summer night, Hillary's fate changed. She tracked down Wally the pickpocket, a terribly difficult man to find.

And Hillary's wish came true.

The day Hillary was promoted to Secret Agent was the happiest day of her life.

She was so happy, she was happier than the time she made history as the first female valedictorian to recite Newton.

She was so happy, she was happier than the time Billy the Cook counter proposed.

She was even happier than the time she won
Secretary of Skate.

Hillary's first assignment was a hard one. Her new boss had given her a tough nut to crack.

It was the case of the missing hotdog.

The hotdog belonged to Hugh Heffner, Curator of the Playboy Mansion in Los Angeles.

On-site survellience cameras first misled them to think they had caught the culprit hiding the goods in his pants.

But upon further inspection, the privates realized the crook was still at large.

Hillary and Macy, who was now Secret Sidekick, scoped out the mansion's lay of the land.

Was the thief still on the premises? Did the thief escape? Did the thief leave any clues at the gate?

Hillary and Macy came up with nothing, and they approached the mansion to meet the Curator himself.

"I knew this was no matter for the police," Hugh Heffner said. "I needed private eyes because everyone and everything here goes down in secret."

"Tell us about the hotdog," Hillary ordered.

"Gladly," Hugh said. "I bought that hotdog at a cart in Beverly Hills. It was the biggest, most beautiful hotdog I had ever seen."

"I paid the vendor its worth," he continued. "10,000 dollars."

Hugh took a puff from his pipe. "But it's not the hotdog's monetary value I miss. It's its sentimental value. You see, the hotdog compensates for my personal shortcomings."

"Show me the scene of the crime," said Hillary.

"Follow me," said Hugh, and he led the two privates through a swinging party to reach his gallery.

"Who are these guests?" Hillary asked.

"On top of the bunnies, mostly celebrities," Hugh replied. "I only invite famous people to my parties."

"Interesting…" thought Hillary.

When they reached the gallery, Hugh showed Hillary a giant empty bun.

"Hmmm," said Hillary. "When did you last see the hotdog?"

"It was with me this morning when I woke up," Hugh told her.

Hillary observed the display case. "No broken glass. No fingerprints. No code or lock."

"That's correct," Hugh responded. "Our thief must be very agile."

"Look there!" Hillary exclaimed. "The painting on the wall!"

She led Macy to a giant painting of swirls and strokes.

"Why, this painting is splattered." Macy observed.

"Exactly!" declared Hillary. "Relish. Mustard. Diced onions. Ketchup. Sauerkraut. Chili. These are exactly the clues we are looking for!"

"If we find the source of the condiments, we find the thief." Hillary turned to Hugh. "Which guests left tonight's party early?"

Hugh gave her six names.

Case Report

Suspect 1: Bernie Bathers

Condiment in question: The Relish

Operation: The private eyes entered suspect's house. There they proceeded secretly to the bathroom, following the sound of running water and singing.

Upon secret entry, they saw suspect in the bath, scrubbing his back with relish.

It appears suspect mixes relish with his bath salt.

Conclusion:

Case Report - continued

Suspect 2: Donald Trumpf

Condiment in question: The Mustard

Operation: The private eyes located suspect at the Bully Fight Saloon. Privates secretly cased the bar to find Sammy the Tender, Meggy the Moderator, and suspect himself riding a mechanical golden elephant.

It was concluded the suspect was using the mustard to squirt gold colored glop as a riding lubricant.

Conclusion:

Case Report - continued

Suspect 3: Sarah Pallin

Condiment in question: The Diced Onions

Operation: The private eyes located suspect on a platform. Suspect was on the path to execute a turkey.

Suspect was throwing diced onions at turkey bystanders. Suspect seemed to be using onions for a tear jerk effect.

Conclusion:

Case Report - continued

Suspect 4: Chris Crissy

Condiment in question: The Ketchup

Operation: The private eyes tracked down suspect in his playroom. Suspect was playing cars on his train table.

Suspect used ketchup as toy blood which was all over his cars and his hands.

Conclusion:

Case Report - continued

<u>Suspect 5:</u> Arnold Schwarzenagger

<u>Condiment in question:</u> The Sauerkraut

<u>Operation:</u> Secret Agent decided to try a new technique, which was to disguise herself and approach suspect directly. Agent disguised herself as reporter.

Agent interrogated suspect at his office. Agent learned that suspect does not eat sauerkraut as a topping.

It was determined suspect eats sauerkraut as finger food.

<u>Conclusion:</u>

Case Report - continued

Suspect 6: **Bengassi Committee**

Condiment in question: **The Chili**

Operation: Secret Agent crashed suspect's dinner in a game of cat and mouse.

With no choice but to play along, Agent sat for supper. As the meal wore on, Agent held her breath for something telling to transpire.

But in the end, Agent concluded suspect consumed chili for the sake of gas alone.

Conclusion:

"That clears our six suspects," Hillary said.

"Should we go home?" Macy asked.

Hillary snapped her fingers. "Wait! I've got it! What if we've been looking for the wrong topping. In fact, what if the clue we're looking for isn't a topping at all. Macy, follow me!"

Hillary led Macy to the Dog n Suds. "It was right before our eyes the whole time. Macy, where do hotdog thieves hide themselves?"

"Why, among other hotdog lovers," Macy exclaimed.

"Exactly! And what do hotdog lovers drink?" Hillary answered her own question. "Beer, of course! And the missing hotdog is huge! So, whoever has drunk the most beer at Dog n Suds is our man!"

"And there she is," Hillary said. "Elizabeth Warden, I should have known it was you. You're under arrest for stealing a hotdog."

That night after the commotion, Hillary walked home.

Her first case was a success. Warden was behind bars. Her boss was happy. Hugh had closure.

It started to drizzle.

"I've done good," Hillary told herself. She knew Secret Agent was the job for her.

Hillary yawned, "Tonight I will sleep a long, deep sleep. I have to…"

"…because tomorrow," she thought, "it's the case of the missing umbrella."

True story: In 1998, Hillary Clinton appeared at the Concourse Hotel in Madison, Wisconsin to endorse Senator Russ Feingold in his '98 campaign. There was a torrential downpour and Hillary's secret service personnel were ill-prepared; they needed an umbrella to hold over the first lady as they escorted her in. I was at the hotel to hear her speak, and I loaned them my umbrella. I was excited to get my umbrella back so I could keep it forever and tell its story. Unfortunately, Hillary's secret service never gave me my umbrella back.

About the author: Beth Schaefer has been writing comedy since 2013 at the age of 38. She founded her publishing company Books on a Whim that same year. Beth's books are primarily humor, but she is also branching into family-centered genres and nonfiction.

About the illustrator: Hasby Mubarok has been drawing since he was a child. He graduated with a degree in Visual Design at the Indonesian Institute of Art. At 30-years-old, Hasby is an up-and-coming artist in Indonesia, who frequently exhibits at art expositions. He is currently publishing his first comic strip "Madura dalam Canda."

Contact:
Visit BooksOnAWhim.com
Email info@BooksOnAWhim.com
Or write:
Books on a Whim
PO Box 5066
Evanston, IL
60204-5066

Secret Agent Hillary and the Case of the Missing Hotdog
goes well with:

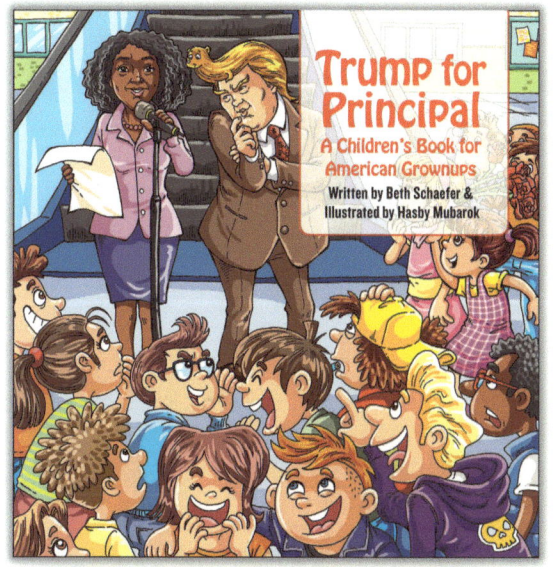

Trump for Principal: A Children's Book for American Grownups
(The updated 2016 Edition)

Donald Trump is elected grade school principal. From the weasel who is his hair to his chocolate milk martini, from the PTA riot to duck duck goose with the klan; from the school nurse on his lap to the crowning of Mr. America: See what chaos ensues!

Hilarious cartoons on every page! FULL COLOR. Appropriate for all ages...mostly. Rated PG.

The **Nutty Years of the Jon Stewart Presidency in a Nutshell**

This mock term paper pokes wacky fun across party lines and at a slew of celebrities.

Jon Stewart is elected U.S. President. And boy is it one crazy term!

Beth Schaefer's satirical story is stocked with wordplay, innuendos, celebrity and politician scandals, and spoofs of all sorts of controversies.

If you like wit, edge, pop culture, and absurdity, this is the book for you. Rated R.

More by Beth Schaefer, Books on a Whim:

Sometimes I wish I had a dad (and an Xbox)

This richly illustrated book is customized for children (ages 4-9) who have absent dads. This book portrays a loving variety of kind, paternal men--in the form of teacher, uncle, coach, and more.

This book celebrates the people who are present in a child's life, demonstrating the joy life still affords despite a parent's abandonment. Rated G.

Grade A Papers: The Slap Stack
A funny coffee table book for English teachers and the universe

This collection of funny, refreshingly original fake student papers is complete with custom-made art on nearly every paper. This book pokes friendly fun at the random eccentricities and idiosyncrasies of college teachers and students. Rated PG-13.

Coming soon:
Grade A Papers II: A funny coffee table book for history teachers and the universe

Welcome to the world of Whimsor College. Whimsor is a fictional liberal arts college located in Columbia, Missouri, just north of Shady Lake and east of Bear Creek Trail. Like its predecessor, this collection of quirky fake student papers is rich with custom-made art on nearly every paper. Rated PG.

www.booksonawhim.com

www.ingramcontent.com/pod-product-compliance
Lightning Source LLC
Chambersburg PA
CBHW040057160426
43192CB00002B/94